THE OFFICIAL FAJITA COOKBOOK

THE OFFICIAL FAJITA COOKBOOK

RICHARD L. MILLER

SECOND EDITION REVISED BY T. L. BUSH

Gulf Publishing Company
Houston, Texas

Chapter opening artwork used by permission of Dover Publications, Inc. Artwork selected from the following Dover publications:

ANIMALS
Selected by Jim Harter
Copyright © 1979 by Dover Publications, Inc.

PICTURE SOURCEBOOK FOR COLLAGE AND DECOUPAGE
Edited by Edmund V. Gillon, Jr.
Copyright © 1974 by Dover Publications, Inc.

DESIGNS FROM PRE-COLUMBIAN MEXICO
By Jorge Enciso
Copyright © 1971 by Dover Publications, Inc.

GOODS AND MERCHANDISE: A Cornucopia of Nineteenth-Century Cuts
Compiled and Arrange by William Rowe
Copyright © 1982 by Dover Publications, Inc.

HANDBOOK OF EARLY ADVERTISING ART, Third Edition
By Clarence P. Hornung
Copyright © 1956 by Dover Publications, Inc.

HANDS: A Pictorial Archive from Nineteenth-Century Sources
Selected by Jim Harter
Copyright © 1985 by Dover Publications, Inc.

FOOD AND DRINK: A Pictorial Archive from Nineteenth-Century Sources, Third Revised Edition
Selected by Jim Harter
Copyright © 1979, 1980, 1983 by Dover Publications, Inc.

MEN: A Pictorial Archive From Nineteenth-Century Sources
Selected by Jim Harter
Copyright © 1980 Dover Publications, Inc.

HARTER'S PICTURE ARCHIVE
Edited by Jim Harter
Copyright © 1978 by Dover Publications, Inc.

Gulf Publishing Company
Book Division
P.O. Box 2608 ☐ Houston, Texas 77252-2608

Library of Congress Cataloging-in-Publication Data
Miller, Richard L., 1947–
    The official fajita cookbook / by Richard L. Miller and T. L. Bush.
        p.   cm.
    Includes index.
    ISBN 0-87719-289-8
    1. Fajitas.   I. Bush, T. L., 1947–   . II. Title.
TX740.M45   1996
641.5972—dc20   96-11574
                                                        CIP

Book design by Walter Horton Design

Printed in the United States of America

THIS BOOK IS FOR
CISCO, AURORA, JOHNSON, TAQUITCHE,
THE CREATURE FROM THE BLACK LAGOON,
AND, OF COURSE,
STEPHANIE

Contents

PREFACE

This book is the culmination of approximately seventeen years of research into fajitas, frijoles *al charro*, *barbacoa de cabeza*, *cabrito al pastor*, Corona Extra, pachuco Spanish, and other cultural items indigenous to South Texas and the border area. The project began while on a vacation courtesy of the U.S. Army at Fort Sam Houston in San Antonio in 1970 and continued in 1974 at Corpus Christi and points south.

My associates and I made numerous visits to restaurants, cantinas, bars, grills, bar-and-grills, backyard barbecues, beachfront get-togethers, gas stations, roadside stands, cookoffs, cookouts, and cookins — all in pursuit of the ultimate fajita, all in the name of science.

No restaurant was too expensive, no location too impossible to check out, no *barbacoa* too greasy, no fajita too tough. In my travels, I tasted fajitas that tasted like fajitas (Matamoros), like barbecue (somewhere near McAllen), like regular sirloin (in Houston), and like Spam (sorry, Seattle). I've heard Mexican waiters claim that their restaurant serves only *real* Mexican food (Boston), the best fajitas in the world (San Antonio), and *cabrito* fajitas (Saltillo).

I have traveled routes 77, 83, 277, 281, 48, 100, 107, I-70, I-80, I-90, I-35, I-45, I-5, I-30, I-94, I-95, I-495, and the New York subway, all in my search for the definitive fajita.

Notes were taken on the backs of matchbooks; inside textbooks; on shirt-sleeves, napkins, tablecloths, newspapers; in U.S. Army pocket notebooks, Nu-Bound Narrow-Ruled Three Subject Notebooks, and the exceedingly rare Executive Memo Book No. 7546. The legible notes were transferred to disk on an Apple III computer. The illegible notes were retained and will someday form the basis for a novel.

—*Richard L. Miller*

INTRODUCTION

Fajitas, also known as skirt steaks or flank steaks, became quite popular during the 1980s. Skirt steaks are taken from the rib area—specifically, the diaphragm. The meat is somewhat tough, requiring tenderizing and flavoring. Part of the mystique of grilled fajitas lies in the variety of marinades used: Italian dressing, lime juice, wine, even rum.

By the mid-1980s, fajita cookoffs had become popular, with amateur chefs and restaurateurs alike competing for the best skirt steaks or marinade.

Fajita popularity reached a new stage in 1985 with the opening of restaurants headlining fajitas. Places with names like Fajitaville and Fajita Willie's appeared, and establishments began offering fajita tacos as a specialty fast food. One national chain, Jack in the Box, offered the fajita pita and committed a national television ad campaign to the product.

At the supermarket, prices for skirt steak shot up from $0.49 a pound in 1975 to well over $2.00 a pound in 1985 and up to $4.00 a pound in 1995.

In 1986, the word started to take on new meaning as restaurants bagan offering chicken and pork "fajitas." Customers assumed that the term referred not to the cut of meat but rather to the way it was grilled. That being the case, "fajita-style catfish" couldn't be far off.

This book is about fajitas, along with several of the foods that seem to go well with them. It discusses the origins of grilled skirt steaks and the jump from a local delicacy to national status and even gives some good recipes for grilling them yourself, in your own backyard.

The book is directed to anyone who ever had—or wanted—the opportunity to try grilled fajitas the way they are prepared in their original setting, South Texas.

RIGIN OF THE FAJITA

Fajita means "little belt" or "sash" in Spanish, and the steak does resemble a cummerbund. For years, meat markets in the North referred to the cut of meat taken from the diaphragm as the "skirt," apparently because it divided the heart and lungs from the innards at a midpoint on the steer.

There are two types of fajitas. Outside skirt steaks are taken from the diaphragm muscle itself on the inside surface of the short plate in the forequarter. Inside skirt steaks are taken from the secondary flank muscle on the inside part of the flank in the hindquarter. The inner fajita is said to be somewhat tastier. Trail bosses usually asked for *la faja de adentro* rather than the tougher outside skirt.

Each steer has only two inside and two outside skirts—about eight pounds of fajitas. Nonetheless, for decades skirt steaks were not a particularly popular cut. In fact, meat markets in the North routinely ground the fajitas and added them to hamburger. It is entirely possible that one of McDonald's first hamburgers may in fact have been a fajitaburger.

Popular history has it that fajitas are a recent invention, served up *al pastor* by Mexican workers on South Texas ranches. Many newspaper food editors refer to this story and date the beginning of grilled skirt steaks to the late 1930s or early 1940s.

This theory holds that fajitas became popular somewhat later, in an area bordered by the King Ranch to the east, the Rio Grande to the south and west, and the Nueces River to the north. According to this view, the barren chaparral surrounding towns like Freer, Benavides, Hebbronville, and Falfurrias is the original home of grilled fajitas.

Laborers working on ranches in this desolate area were given skirt steaks as partial payment, along with other less popular parts of the steer such as the head, stomach, and hide. The laborers used other recipes for the head and stomach and tenderized the skirt steaks by pounding with stones, followed by grilling directly on the surface of hot coals. This didn't result in the damage one might expect—the thin membrane covering the skirt steak kept the moisture inside the meat and prevented it from drying out. After the fajitas were removed from the coals, the membrane was peeled away and the fajitas were eaten. One thing is certain—fajitas cooked this way are decidedly *smokier* than those prepared any other way.

Actually, the practice of marinating then grilling the tough skirt steak may have begun much earlier than that. According to food historian Juanita Garza of Pan American University, the first fajitas were grilled in the villages and small border towns along the Rio Grande around the turn of the century.

The world of the Rio Grande Valley was considerably different at the turn of the century than it is today: mesquite and thornbrush covered most of the sandy, arid land, while the river could be depended upon only to overflow its banks at least once a year.

During the first decade of the twentieth century, land developers from the North began setting up a string of Anglo settlements at what they considered a safe distance from the river—towns like Donna, San Benito, and San Juan (all founded in 1904), Harlingen and McAllen (1905), Mercedes (1906), and La Feria (1909).

At the time there were also a number of small Mexican settlements much closer to the river, with names like Santa Maria, Los Indios, La Paloma, and Progresso, all predating the northern developers by decades. Thirty-eight years into the new century, a Works Progress Administration writer described these settlements: "Oil lamps and flickering tallow wicks gleam in the windows of homes and store buildings, and much of the family cooking is done over charcoal braziers in the yards. Many of the houses are mere *jacales* of mud and sticks, but few are so humble that a flowering potted plant or two does not rest on a little bench beside the doorstep" (*WPA Guide to Texas*, Austin: Texas Monthly Press, 1986, p. 465).

There is little doubt that some of the first fajitas were grilled on the charcoal braziers in these little border villages.

By the 1930s, the average Texan still hadn't discovered fajitas. Oddly enough, skirt steaks were already enjoying a popularity of sorts in, of all places, Depression-era Vermont. Back then, when every cut of meat counted, cooks would take the tough skirt steak, trim it down, marinate it, then wrap it around a garnish such as potatoes, carrots, and onions. But instead of grilling it, the New Englanders would place the skirt steak in a pot as a roast.

While it's not certain when the first fajitas appeared in Matamoros, the first restaurant on the U.S. side to serve them was probably Pharr's Roundup Restaurant in 1972. It had, in effect, taken seventy years for grilled fajitas to travel the short distance from the village's charcoal brazier to the restaurant, perhaps twelve miles away. It would take only another thirteen years before grilled fajitas became popular in the rest of the country.

(For more information, see Mary K. Sweeten and Homer Recio, *Fajitas South Texas Style*, College Station: Agricultural Extension Service, Texas A&M University, 1985, p. 6.)

HOW TO EAT A FAJITA

While fajitas served "steak style" can be easily eaten with a fork, skirt steaks with tacos can be extremely messy: so here you are, at a fajita restaurant, ordering a half-pound combo platter and a margarita to wash it all down. While waiting for your number to be called, you walk over to the salad bar and pick up two or three small containers of salsa. The order arrives, hot and sizzling, with a foil-wrapped roll of warm flour tortillas and a large helping of cold guacamole.

The first thing that usually happens is that you get your sleeve into something: fajitas, salsa, or guacamole. Of the three, guacamole probably looks the worst.

Fajitas are messy. That is part of their popularity. The dishes are occasionally greasy, tending to splatter salsa and guacamole *everywhere*, and anyone without a sturdy napkin is in for a rough time indeed.

You won't mind the mess and bother once you've assembled and tasted a fajita. There are a million ways to eat fajitas. Only one is presented here—a method that will ensure the least amount of mess and the greatest degree of taste.

Open up the foil-covered tortillas. Remove a single tortilla and reseal. Take the knife and lay down a thin layer of guacamole on the tortilla. Sprinkle a few leaves of cilantro on top of the guacamole. Lay down two or three strips of fajita steak. Drizzle some salsa or pico de gallo over the steaks. Fold the tortilla lengthwise into a burrito shape, leaving a flap at the bottom. Curl the bottom flap over to prevent grease, salsa, and pico de gallo from leaking onto your clothing.

Congratulations. You now have a fajita taco.

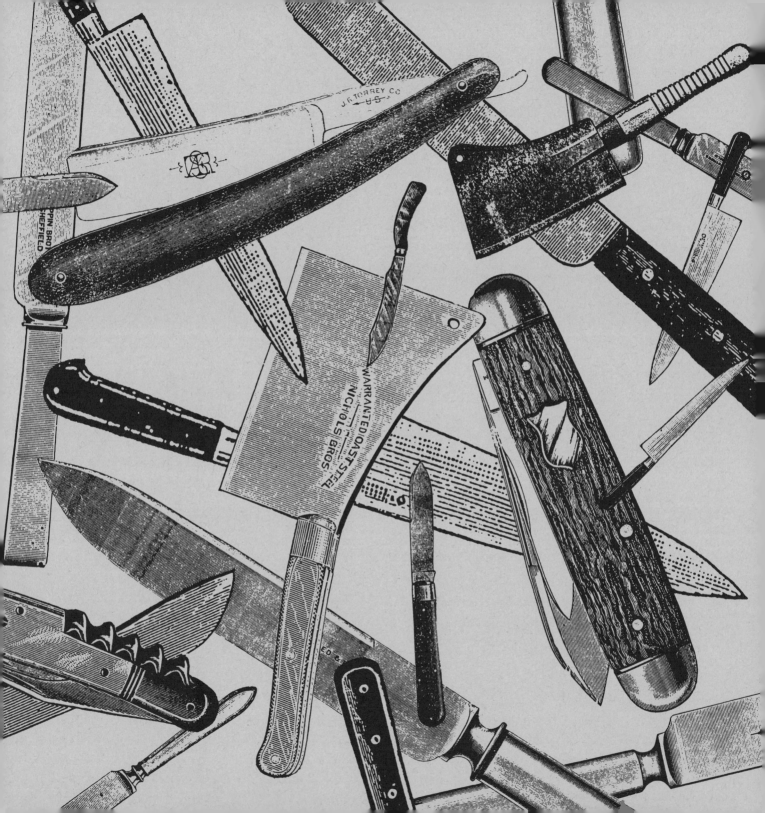

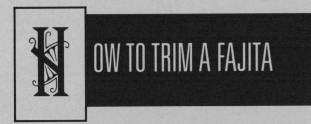OW TO TRIM A FAJITA

Fajitas are usually purchased with some fat and membrane still covering the meat. You should remove most of the fat, but not all, leaving some for added flavor.

1. Lay the fajita on a nonporous cutting board and, using a knife, remove the fat. This is a somewhat tedious process, since the fat is usually contained in small pockets. My female friend refers to this as "fajita cellulite." Discard the fat.

2. Skirt steak muscle is covered with a tough membrane that must be removed. The trick is to grab the membrane with one hand and slide the knife beneath it, cutting as you go. Some fajita chefs actually use surgeon's scissors; the rounded blade makes the job go faster.

3. By this time, you should have a skinned, trimmed fajita before you. Now for the tenderizing process. Studiously ignore anyone who suggests using a meat mallet. This barbaric method merely smashes the meat into a non-recognizable pulp. Also ignore those who reach for the meat tenderizer. Tenderizers work much like mallets, replacing sheer force with enzymes—the result is the same. There *is* a better way.

Using a sharp paring knife, make a number of 1-inch slits in the meat, cutting both with and against the grain. This cuts the muscle fiber and effectively reduces toughness. It also allows the marinade to permeate the meat. Follow up by using a fork to puncture the meat thoroughly.

An alternate method involves cubing—cutting or chopping the skirt steak *across* the grain in a crisscross pattern. First make a series of parallel cuts against the grain, all the way across the steak. Then repeat the series of cuts at an angle to the first group.

4. Optional: if you *must* use a tenderizer, this is the time. Place a small amount of tenderizer in a cup of warm water and pour it on the meat. Let sit for 15 minutes per side.

5. Place the meat in the marinade of choice (see Recipes: Marinades) in a covered dish and refrigerate for at least an hour.

Your skirt steak is now ready for any of the recipes in this book.

THE SECRET INGREDIENTS

CILANTRO

Most of the 340-odd fast-food chains offer some form of fajita steak, whether as a burger ("Just say 'Fajitaburger'!"), Fajita McNuggets, Fajita-in-a-Pita, Breakfast Fajita Taquito, or Fajita 'n Egg Breakfast. Most will fail.

The reason won't be the fajita taste itself. Food scientists are certainly able to take a slab of cheap chuck or round and accurately reproduce the tangy taste of true fajita; at the very least, they can mask the taste of regular beef by adding copious amounts of onions and garlic.

Nor will errors in design be the downfall of typical fast-food fajitas. The cooks can grill up some regular beef from *any* part of the cow, throw in hot sauce, cheese, onions, and lettuce, put it in a Middle Eastern invention called a pita pocket, and declare that it's a fajita. Never mind that fajitas traditionally were not served with lettuce, cheese, sour cream, or even sautéed onions—and they certainly were never dished up in a pita pocket.

No, fast-food fajitas will probably fail because of the lack of the secret ingredient: cilantro. Cilantro is also known as coriander and Chinese parsley. It is sold as tiny, yellow seeds

and also as a bright yellow-green leaf that resembles flat-leaf parsley. The seeds must be crushed to release the flavor. When using the leaves, be sure to discard the tough lower stem. The leaves must be kept free from moisture or they will decay. The pungent, warm to hot flavor of the herb is the key ingredient in the majority of the recipes in this book and is as critical to the taste of fajitas as guacamole.

In the mid-1930s, candy manufacturers placed coriander seeds in the center of "jaw breakers." Ten years later American servicemen stationed in India tried local cuisine flavored with *dhuma*. In the early 1940s, Mexican laborers flavored chicken, stews, and grilled steaks with *cothamille* leaves, common in Mexico. Regardless of the name or origin, the herb was the same: *Coriandrum sativum*, also known as cilantro.

This little (18-inch tall) shrub is absolutely essential to a number of delicious dishes: gingered carrots, lemon lentils, lemon sole Yucatán style, marinated raw salmon, Oriental bluefish, tempura, Vietnamese noodles, baked stuffed fish, pork with fennel seeds, buckwheat noodles, sesame chicken, flounder ceviche, Indonesian pork saté, tandoori chicken, steamed artichokes, roasts, clams, and, of course, fajitas.

Cilantro works well only when it is fresh. Therefore, if you're grilling the fajitas yourself, buy the little shrub at your nearest farmer's market. Check to see that the leaves are green

▼▼▼▼▼▼▼▼▼▼▼▼▼▼▼▼▼▼▼▼▼▼▼▼▼▼▼▼▼▼▼▼▼▼▼

and firm — cilantro loses its flavor when dry. So watch out for the brown leaves; they won't be as tasty.

You may also consider growing your own cilantro. Purchase the seeds and plant in the late spring. They need darkness to germinate, but later will survive full sunshine. You can start new plants about every three weeks. Cilantro will grow about two feet tall. When harvesting the cilantro, cut only the leaves. Remember, cilantro is an annual and won't survive the winter.

MESQUITE

There is a rumor that fajitas, to taste like fajitas, should be grilled over mesquite. The rumor is only partially true. Fact is, fajitas properly marinated taste great broiled in an oven using natural gas. Of course, the connoisseurs among you who demand the finest probably should look into mesquite grilling. Fajitas cooked over mesquite *do* taste slightly better.

Mesquite and South Texas seem to go together. While the Texas Hill Country around Austin boasted live oak, cedar, pecans, and an occasional stand of cypress, South Texas seemed to be an unending expanse of chaparral — pure brush country.

When traveler William A. McClintock visited South Texas in 1846, he wrote that "there is nothing of the vegitible world on the rio grand but what is armed with weapons of defence and offence," including a variety of "pricks, thorns, or burs."

Another traveler, William B. DeWees, who had the opportunity to see the vast stretch of land between San Antonio and the Rio Grande, wrote that the area was "covered with shrubs, musquit trees, and prickly pear . . . the road is ofttimes completely hedged in for miles by long rows of prickly pear . . . all the shrubbery throughout this country is covered with thorns" (Walter L. Buenger, ed., *Texas History*, Boston: American Press, 1983, p. 156).

That area is not too different today. Mesquite and prickly pear still seem to predominate in the vast open areas between San Antonio and the border. In fact, there seems to be *more* mesquite than ever before.

In 1850, during William McClintock's tour, the mesquite in South Texas was generally concentrated along the Rio Grande in a band only

twenty-five to fifty miles deep. By 1950 it had largely taken over the entire southern half of the state, extending in an almost unbroken band from Dalhart in the Panhandle to Brownsville and from Red Bluff, near the New Mexico border, to Schulenburg, not far from Houston.

Now, mesquite is not an environmentally useless plant; its roots go deep to help stop erosion and it produces a sugar-rich pod that cattle and wild animals seem fond of. In fact, the cattle and their alimentary tracts are the reason for the spread of mesquite; wherever the cattle wandered, so went the seeds, plus an amount of fertilizer to help the tree grow.

Settlers moving into the area first tried to subdue the tree, then gave up and learned to live with it, using the wood to make everything from railroad ties to furniture. The Indians, however, had made an *exhaustive* study of mesquite—they used the tree to make such things as candy, bread, and even an intoxicating brew.

They also knew how to turn the mesquite into good, clean-burning charcoal. First they covered the mesquite chips with mud-coated straw to form a sort of kiln. Then they ignited the wood and allowed it to smolder. Using this process, they could produce remarkably good charcoal that burns at a rather hot 800 to 1,000° F.

Foods can be grilled over regular mesquite, but the resin causes the fire to pop and crackle. A large log of burning mesquite is, in fact, a show in itself, resembling not so much a peaceful campfire or fireplace as something out of *Star Wars.* Those who roast hot dogs over the open flame on a gas range are familiar with the effect.

Since the mid-1980s, there has been a demand for mesquite surpassing all reason. South Texas farmers and ranchers who once would have treated their friendly mesquite trees to a shower of herbicide now *charge* to have them removed. By 1986, $3.00 to $6.00 a cord was the average price charged to cart the mesquite off. Nevertheless, it was a steal; entrepreneurs all over Texas chopped the mesquite into little chips, then sold the chips to wholesalers for $1.50 per small bag. The wholesalers then sold the chips to retailers for about $2.00 a bag. By the time the mesquite reached the public in, say, Manhattan, the bags of chips were fetching upward of $3.00 each.

All this may change. Someone in California discovered that the Texans have traditionally not used mesquite to grill after all. Instead they used pecan. "Makes the meat taste just a little better," the Californians were told. By 1987, a rush on pecan was developing.

In addition, near San Antonio there is a rancher who plans to start a rumor that his Mexican ranch hands traditionally smoked their fajitas over grapevine. It seems there is this area out on his back forty that he needs cleared.

If you live in the northern tier of states and *must* have mesquite for your grill, simply venture out into the nearest woods and find some black locust. It's a cousin of the mesquite; the grilling characteristics are probably similar.

MARINADE

The marinade is a liquid designed to tenderize meat. If it adds flavor, so much the better. There are a lot of good tenderizers in the plant world—among them, pineapple, citrus fruits, and papaya. The acetic acid found in ordinary vinegar is a terrific tenderizer, but not many people care for the sharp taste.

When the Mexican ranch hands first began grilling fajitas, it is doubtful that they used fruit juice to tenderize a few pounds of steak. More likely, they poked numerous holes in the meat with knives. They wanted to save the limes for their afternoon tequila.

So, for the most part, marinades have evolved into just a flavoring agent. But they are *subtle* flavoring agents. In the intense heat of a charcoal fire, many things boil off, leaving few basic flavors intact. In fact, some flavors that are imparted to the meat have little resemblance to the original pregrilling ingredients. Most common examples involve liquors. A heady marinade containing Cointreau or Grand Marnier grills out as burnt orange—interesting with duck and chicken, but it makes a fajita taste like some sort of strange candy.

There is a continuing controversy over whether limes should be used in marinades. While I think that limes belong only in margaritas, there are otherwise sane persons who use them in marinades. In fact, there are a great number of people who believe limes are essential to fajita marinade. However, there are an equal number who believe that soy sauce is the ingredient that makes the difference. Others favor light vinegars, wines, and oils; still others believe that ordinary Italian dressing is all that is necessary to make a terrific marinade. Worse, I suspect that one restaurant in the Rio Grande Valley famous for its fajitas uses only water and meat tenderizer.

There are as many ways to fix fajitas as there are marinades. Add something new to the marinade and you have an entirely new recipe. I've included marinades of every type. There are recipes based on lime, on soy, and on oil/wine/vinegar, as well as a guide for those who want to expand on a basic marinade recipe—experiment, taste, and enjoy!

MARINADES

BASIC FAJITA PREPARATION

Trim your skirt steak as instructed in the chapter "How to Trim a Fajita" before using these marinades. After marinating, the fajita meat should be cut into six-inch lengths and either grilled outside on a charcoal grill or cooked in a heavy skillet over high heat. Cook about 3 to 5 minutes on each side, turning the meat once. After the meat is cooked, cut on the diagonal into thin strips and serve with your favorite fajita condiments.

SPICY ORIENTAL MARINADE

This is a great marinade for those who want to fix fajitas at the spur of the moment because overnight refrigeration is not required.

1/2 CUP SOY SAUCE

1/4 CUP VINEGAR

1/4 CUP WATER

1 TABLESPOON SUGAR

1 TABLESPOON CHILI POWDER

1 TEASPOON GARLIC POWDER

1 TEASPOON GROUND GINGER

Mix all of the ingredients. Coat the meat with the mixture. Cover tightly and refrigerate 3 or 4 hours. Makes about 1 cup.

BEER MARINADE

For some reason, people like to throw beer on grilling food. I suspect that the practice originated in the 1960s when backyard barbecuing became popular—someone probably spilled a can of Falstaff onto the hot coals by accident, thus producing enormous amounts of smoke and ash, making the steaks taste like the inside of a wood-burning stove. Since the "hickory flavor" was just catching on about that time, the guests applauded the effort. The cook mistakenly thought the beer was the thing that did the trick. That, perhaps, is the single reason a great variety of beers lasted as long as they did. If people didn't drink them, they could at least throw them into the barbecue.

1/2 CUP COTTONSEED OIL

1/2 12-OUNCE CAN BEER

1/4 CUP WINE VINEGAR

1 TEASPOON SALT

1 TEASPOON PEPPER

1 TABLESPOON CILANTRO, CHOPPED

1 TEASPOON GARLIC, MINCED

Mix all of the ingredients and pour over the fajita meat. Cover tightly and refrigerate for 4 hours. Makes about 1½ cups.

VARIATIONS OF BEER MARINADE

For Oriental flavor, add 2 tablespoons of teriyaki sauce. For Hawaiian flavor, use ½ cup pineapple juice instead of the beer.

OLIVE OIL AND LEMON MARINADE

1 CLOVE GARLIC, CRUSHED
2 TABLESPOONS LEMON JUICE
1 CUP OLIVE OIL
1 TEASPOON OREGANO

Mix all of the ingredients. Place the steak in the marinade, cover tightly, and let stand at room temperature for 2 to 3 hours. Makes about 1 cup.

LIME MARINADE

1 CUP BEEF BROTH (INSTANT BOUILLON IS FINE)
2 TABLESPOONS LIME JUICE
3 TABLESPOONS WORCESTERSHIRE SAUCE
1 CLOVE GARLIC, MINCED
1 TABLESPOON BROWN SUGAR
1 TABLESPOON CILANTRO, CHOPPED

Mix all of the ingredients. Coat the fajita meat with the marinade and refrigerate overnight. Makes about 1½ cups.

WINE VINEGAR MARINADE

1/3 CUP WINE VINEGAR
3 TABLESPOONS OLIVE OIL
2 TABLESPOONS HONEY
1 TEASPOON GARLIC POWDER
2 TEASPOONS CILANTRO, CHOPPED

Mix all of the ingredients. Coat the fajita meat with the marinade and refrigerate overnight. Makes about ⅔ cup.

SWEET MARINADE

Some people marinate their steaks in liquor. Interestingly, some liquors actually make the fajitas taste better. The most common addition seems to be rum. For one thing, it's a sugar-based liquid that, when subjected to intense heat, turns to caramel. Those considering rum should be advised that it's probably better to use brown sugar instead—the effect is about the same and it's cheaper. The problem with using rum and other sweet liquors is that if you use too much you will have *candied* fajitas on your conscience. It is better to grill fajitas marinated in a sugar-based recipe over a lower fire.

1 CUP ORANGE JUICE
1/2 CUP BROWN SUGAR
1/2 CUP WORCESTERSHIRE SAUCE
1/4 CUP VINEGAR
1/4 CUP WATER
1/4 CUP PARSLEY, CHOPPED
3 TEASPOONS GARLIC POWDER
1 TABLESPOON BASIL

Mix the first five ingredients together until they are blended well. Add the remaining ingredients and pour the mixture over the skirt steak. Cover tightly and refrigerate overnight. Makes about 3 cups.

MARINADE TIPS

1. Make sure your fajitas are completely covered by the marinade.

2. The longer you leave the fajitas in the marinade, the tastier they will be.

3. Salt is not included in most marinade recipes because it has a tendency to draw out the meat juices. It is better to add salt right before you begin cooking your fajitas or after the meat is done.

4. Take marinated meats out of the refrigerator at least 1 to 2 hours before grilling, so that your fajitas will cook evenly.

5. Drain as much of the marinade as possible from the meat before cooking, reserving it to baste your fajitas.

BUT IS IT GOOD FOR YOU?

First the bad news: a diet of fajitas, guacamole, tortillas, and sauteed onions will make you round.

The facts: one tortilla contains about 2 grams protein, 5 grams fat, and 15 grams of carbohydrates for a total of 115 calories. The one ounce of lean skirt steak found in a typical fajita-tortilla combination contains 7 grams protein, 5 grams fat, and zero carbohydrates, equaling about 75 calories. If you include about one-fourth cup of guacamole, add 5 grams of fat and 45 calories.

Pack on sauteed onions and you have another 90 calories, while half a cup of various vegetables adds another 2 grams protein, 5 grams fat, and 25 calories.

Grand total for an ounce of skirt steak with sauteed onions, guacamole, pico de gallo, and one tortilla: 350 calories.

Like sour cream? Too bad. It is almost pure fat: just two tablespoons equals 45 calories.

FAJITAS

Fajitas are incredibly easy to cook and there is a very good reason for this: only a limited number of recipes actually work. Oh, sure, you will find fajita cowboys who broil them up with rum and Coke and whiskey and who-knows-what, but the result is, at best, an acquired taste—sort of like the recipe (which I'm particularly fond of) involving artichoke hearts.

Fact of the matter is, just about any food worth its salt (or lack thereof) engenders a vast number of off-the-wall recipes. In fact, there are more *potential* recipes for fajitas than there are guitar chords in a typical Chet Atkins song. However, the recipes that actually work are equal to the number of chords in the typical Van Halen chartbuster.

Rest assured, they are included in this book—along with a good number of the others—recipes and variations on a terrific theme.

FAJITAS WITH ARTICHOKE HEARTS

1 6-OUNCE JAR OF ARTICHOKE HEARTS, CHOPPED

1/4 CUP OLIVE OIL

1/2 CUP DRY RED WINE

1 TEASPOON ROSEMARY

1 TEASPOON BASIL

1/4 TEASPOON CILANTRO, CHOPPED

1/4 TEASPOON PARSLEY

2 POUNDS SKIRT STEAK

Drain the liquid from the artichoke hearts into a bowl. Reserve the artichokes. Mix the artichoke liquid with all the other ingredients. Pour the marinade over the fajita meat and refrigerate for 1 hour. Remove the meat from the marinade and grill or cook for 4 to 5 minutes on each side. Serve the fajitas with the artichoke hearts. Serves 2–4.

CORN CAKES

Don't put that griddle away when you're done warming those tortillas. Just turn the fire up a little and get ready for some more good eating.

1 15 1/2-OUNCE CAN CORN

3/4 CUP FLOUR

1/2 TEASPOON SALT

2 TABLESPOONS BUTTER (MELTED)

1/2 TEASPOON BAKING POWDER

MILK

Open canned corn and drain off water. Pour corn into a bowl large enough to add other ingredients. Add all other things except milk. Now slowly add milk, mixing as you add it. Add just enough milk to create a pancake-type batter. Fry on your heated griddle like pancakes. Make sure the griddle is oiled to avoid sticking. Serve hot with butter or a good salsa.

PRIMO'S FAJITAS

1 SKIRT STEAK FOR EACH 3 SERVINGS

2 CUPS SOY SAUCE (SUCH AS KIKKOMAN)

2 CUPS WORCESTERSHIRE SAUCE

1/4 CUP PINEAPPLE JUICE

JUICE OF 1 LIME

FLOUR TORTILLAS

OPTIONAL: PICO DE GALLO, BEANS, RICE

Peel off any membrane on the skirt steak. Slice lengthwise so it is no more than ¾ inch thick. Cut into 6-ounce serving portions. For basting: combine soy sauce and Worcestershire with pineapple juice, lime juice, and a pinch of salt. Mix well. Dip steak in mixture. Sear over very high heat, then grill until cooked to your taste, turning occasionally, about 6 to 8 minutes. Brush with basting mixture several times. Slice in thin strips. Wrap in flour tortilla; serve with pico de gallo, beans, and rice. Makes enough basting mixture for 4 steaks.

(Adapted from the *Houston Chronicle*, January 14, 1987)

NATIONAL FAJITAS

1 1/2 POUNDS SKIRT STEAK

1/2 CUP VEGETABLE OIL

1 SMALL ONION, THINLY SLICED

1 GARLIC CLOVE, PRESSED

JUICE OF 1 LIME

2 CHILES, MINCED

8 6-INCH TORTILLAS

Make a marinade of the ingredients and soak the steaks in the refrigerator for at least an hour. When the meat is ready, cut into 6-inch lengths (1½ inches wide). Either grill outside on a charcoal grill or cook in a heavy skillet over high heat. With either method, turn the meat once and cook about 3 to 5 minutes on each side. After the meat is cooked, cut on the diagonal into thin strips.

This dish can be assembled at the table. Put condiments in small bowls. Place warmed tortillas and sizzling meat on separate plates. To assemble, place meat into warm tortillas, cover with choice of toppings, roll, and eat with your hands. Serves 4.

(Adapted from Linda West Eckhardt, *An American Gumbo: Affordable Cuisine for the Everyday Gourmet*, Austin: Texas Monthly Press, 1983, p. 94)

SIDE KICKS

Every hero has a side kick and I think fajitas are no exception. This is a nice *botana* (snack) that goes quite well with fajitas. I like to make this on the grill while I'm doing my fajitas.

2 1/2 POUNDS ZUCCHINI (SLICED)

2 ONIONS (THINLY SLICED)

3 MEDIUM TOMATOES (PEELED AND SLICED)

1 TEASPOON SALT

1/2 TEASPOON PEPPER

1/2 TEASPOON DRIED BASIL

1/2 TEASPOON OREGANO

2 TABLESPOONS BUTTER

With double thickness aluminum foil, make a large square. Place all the vegetables into the center of the foil. Sprinkle with the seasonings and add butter. Fold and seal the foil by rolling the edges together. Grill over a medium-hot fire for about 30 minutes. You need to shake the foil once in a while to keep the juices mixing.

FAKE FAJITAS

Here's a no-brainer. What do you do if you can't find fajitas in your meat department? Fake it!

Find a nice 2 pound, boneless, chuck arm roast, about 3 or 4 inches thick works fine. To assist in tenderizing, slice the roast across the grain in slices about 1/2-inch thick. Trim off all the fat. Salt, pepper, and season to your own taste. Soak in your favorite marinate about an hour. Drain off juice and cook about 3 minutes per side in a lightly oiled fry pan. When done serve on tortillas and cover with your favorite toppings.

ONE COOL SALAD

No matter when you serve fajitas, summer or winter, it's always nice to have a refreshing salad. This one is simple and good.

6 MEDIUM TOMATOES (CUT INTO CHUNKS)

1 GREEN PEPPER (CHOPPED)

1 LARGE ONION (SLICED)

1/4 CUP SUGAR

2/3 CUP VINEGAR

2/3 CUP WATER

SALT TO TASTE

Put tomatoes, green peppers, and onions into a large bowl. Pour on sugar and gently stir. Let stand for 30 minutes. Stir in remaining ingredients and refrigerate at least four hours before serving.

OUTLAW FAJITAS

Jim Lane of Fort Worth won an award for this recipe at the Pioneer Days Fajita Cookoff in Fort Worth — using commercial "fajita seasoning."

5 POUNDS SKIRT STEAK

FAJITA SEASONING (JIMENEZ IS EXCELLENT)

20 LIMES

1 QUART BEER

1 JAR PICKAPEPPA SAUCE

1 JAR WOODY'S BARBECUE SAUCE

1 TABLESPOON LAWRY'S SEASONED SALT, OR TO TASTE

1 TABLESPOON PEPPER, OR TO TASTE

6 ONIONS, CUT IN WEDGES

Sprinkle the fajita seasoning and squeeze the lime juice over the meat, then place in a pan with the lime peels. Cover with beer and add Pickapeppa and Woody's barbecue sauce along with seasoned salt and pepper. Let sit 24 hours.

Place the steaks on a grill over a mesquite fire. Turn frequently, basting the meat with marinade. Add the onion wedges and cover. Cook for 10 to 15 minutes.

When done, cut the fajitas in 4-inch-long strips, then add the marinade and reheat. Serves 20.

(Adapted from Ann Ruff and Austin West, *Cookoffs!*, Austin: Texas Monthly Press, 1984, p. 144)

▼▼▼▼▼▼▼▼▼▼▼▼▼▼▼▼▼▼▼▼▼▼▼▼▼▼▼▼

VENISON FAJITAS

Texas is not only beef and beans. Although they're not very big, deer are excellent eating if done right. This is about the best marinade I have run cross if you think venison is too gamey.

1 ONION (CHOPPED FINE)

1 DICED CARROT

1 CUP CIDER

1 TEASPOON PAPRIKA

1 CLOVE GARLIC (CRUSHED)

1 BAY LEAF

1/4 TEASPOON NUTMEG

1/2 TEASPOON DRY MUSTARD

2 TABLESPOONS ORANGE JUICE

JUICE FROM ONE LEMON

Combine all the ingredients in a sauce pan and slowly bring to a boil. Let boil for 7 minutes and let cool. Use to marinate venison strips over night. Remove venison and grill on both sides until done.

If you are not a hunter, you will need to contact a butcher shop that processes wild game for hunters. They probably can't sell you the meat but I'll bet they can help you get some.

Prepare the venison just as you would regular skirt steak. Serve this as you would any other fajita and enjoy.

FAST EDDIE'S FAJITAS

In 1985 Fast Eddie's, a restaurant in the Valley town of Port Isabel, won a fajita cookoff in Austin—and did it without using one lime.

3 POUNDS SKIRT STEAK

LEMON-PEPPER SEASONING

GARLIC POWDER

8 OUNCES SOY SAUCE

2 CUPS PINEAPPLE JUICE

1 SMALL CAN CRUSHED PINEAPPLE

2 OUNCES FIGARO LIQUID SMOKE

6 OUNCES WORCESTERSHIRE SAUCE

8 OUNCES CANNED TOMATO SAUCE

1 QUART BEER

2 MEDIUM ONIONS, SLICED

Tenderize the meat with a meat mallet, then sprinkle liberally with lemon-pepper, garlic powder, and soy sauce. Marinate the seasoned meat 24 hours in a mix of the next six ingredients.

Slice the meat into strips about 4 inches long and place in a noncorrosive pan. Cover with sliced onions and cook in the pan over a mesquite fire (do not cook over direct flame). Serves 8 to 12.

(Adapted from Ann Ruff and Austin West, *Cookoffs!*, Austin: Texas Monthly Press, 1984, p. 145)

BASIC WORCESTERSHIRE FAJITAS

MARINADE:

1/3–1/2 CUP BUTTER, MELTED

JUICE OF 1 MEDIUM LEMON

1/4 CUP WORCESTERSHIRE SAUCE

1/4 CUP SOY SAUCE (SUCH AS KIKKOMAN)

CORN TORTILLAS

GUACAMOLE

PICO DE GALLO

PICANTE SAUCE

Slice the meat against the grain in narrow strips not more than ¼ inch thick, then marinate 3 hours. Place the meat on the grill after the coals are white hot and cook for 4 to 8 minutes on each side. Place several strips of meat on each hot corn tortilla, then add guacamole, pico de gallo, and picante sauce.

T.L.'S BOURBON FAJITAS

MARINADE

1/4 CUP BROWN SUGAR

1 TABLESPOON LEMON OR LIME JUICE

1 TEASPOON WORCESTERSHIRE SAUCE

1 5-OUNCE BOTTLE SOY SAUCE

1 1/2 CUPS WATER

1/3 CUP BOURBON

3 POUNDS SKIRT STEAKS

8 TO 10 FLOUR TORTILLAS

YOUR FAVORITE SALSA

Mix the first six things together, tenderize the steak with the back of a knife or by slicing it slightly. Add the meat to the marinade and let stand several hours.

After removing the steaks from the marinade, grill them over a medium-hot fire for about 5 minutes per side. Serve on warm tortillas and cover with salsa.

YRBITF

(YESTERDAY'S ROAST BEEF IS TODAY'S FAJITAS)

Here's the deal. You get home from work only to find you have company. Nothing is thawed and you are expected to be a magician. The only thing you can find is some leftover roast beef in the fridge. No problem!

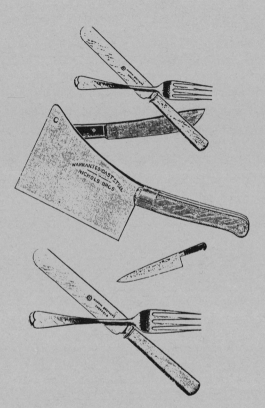

2 POUNDS ROAST BEEF

1 SMALL ONION (CHOPPED)

1/4 CUP CATSUP

2 TEASPOONS CHILI POWDER

1 8-OUNCE CAN CHILI BEANS

1/2 4-OUNCE CAN TOMATO PASTE

GARLIC SALT

1/2 CUP GRATED CHEDDAR CHEESE

BLACK OLIVES

FLOUR TORTILLAS

Trim any fat away from beef and place the beef in a large saucepan. Add other ingredients except cheese and olives. Heat to a low boil. Serve this mixture on warm tortillas. Slice olives, add to cheese, and sprinkle on hot filling.

FAJITAS BAR-B-CUE

2 POUNDS SKIRT STEAK FIXED AS YOU LIKE IT

1/2 CUP CATSUP

1/2 CUP CHOPPED ONION

1 TABLESPOON VINEGAR

1 TABLESPOON MUSTARD

1 TABLESPOON SUGAR

1 TABLESPOON WORCESTERSHIRE SAUCE

Mix everything except the meat, bring to a gentle boil and remove from heat. Place meat on warmed tortillas, spoon desired amount of mixture on meat.

RUM FAJITAS

A fellow named Mike Kutzer of Lajitas, Texas, won top prize at the Fajitas Fandango in Terlingua. The alcohol in the rum boils off and leaves a tasty caramel coating.

2 POUNDS SKIRT STEAK

1 CUP BACARDI LIGHT RUM

18-OUNCE JAR LIQUID CRAB BOIL

Marinate and refrigerate the meat overnight in the rum and crab boil. Cook over mesquite coals. Slice into 4-inch strips. Serves 6.

(Adapted from Ann Ruff and Austin West, *Cookoffs!*, Austin: Texas Monthly Press, 1984, p. 143)

FAJITAS DE TRUETT

3 TO 5 POUNDS FAJITAS

1/2 TEASPOON LEMON PEPPER

1/2 TEASPOON SEASONED SALT

1/2 TEASPOON GARLIC SALT

1/4 TEASPOON MEAT TENDERIZER

1/2 CUP ITALIAN DRESSING

SAUCE:

1 MEDIUM ONION, DICED

1/2 STICK BUTTER OR MARGARINE

1/4 CUP WORCESTERSHIRE SAUCE

1 18-OUNCE BOTTLE SMOKY BARBECUE SAUCE

1/2 CUP KETCHUP

1/2 CAN BEER

1 TABLESPOON BROWN SUGAR (OR TO TASTE)

Remove excess fat and any skin or membrane from the fajitas. Moisten the meat and sprinkle both sides with lemon pepper, seasoned salt, and garlic salt. Cover with a damp cloth for 1 or 2 hours. Approximately 30 minutes before cooking, sprinkle both sides with meat tenderizer and puncture the meat with a dinner fork about every inch. Coat each side with Italian dressing, roll up, and store in a pan, covered with a damp cloth, until ready to cook.

Make the sauce while the meat is marinating. Cook the meat over hot coals approximately 10 minutes on each side—less if the meat is thin. Slice the meat, across the grain, into 1-inch strips. Put the strips back into the pan, pour sauce over, and stir well. Cover the pan and let simmer for 10 to 15 minutes. Add more beer if needed for thinner consistency. Serves 6 to 10.

(Adapted from Junior Service League of McAllen, Texas, *La Piñata*, 1985, p. 311)

FAJITA SALMIS

A salmis was originally a dish prepared from previously roasted foul. Nowadays we know it as leftovers and we do it with any type of meat. So in the unlikely event you have fajitas left over and you would like a different taste, try this.

LEFTOVER FAJITAS

1 BUNCH GREEN ONIONS (CHOPPED)

3 TABLESPOONS FLOUR

1 TABLESPOON LEMON JUICE

2 TABLESPOONS ORANGE JUICE

1 CUP BEEF STOCK

1/4 CUP BUTTER

SALT

DASH CAYENNE

Saute onions in 1/4 cup butter, stir in flour. Cook about 4 minutes then add lemon juice, orange juice, beef stock, salt, to taste, and cayenne. Heat mixture till hot. DO NOT BOIL. Add meat, leaving it in sauce until hot. Put in a hot serving dish and bring on the tortillas.

MARGARITA FAJITAS

This recipe is by Jean Conner of Palestine, Texas, who won second place at the 1984 Texas Beef Cookoff. It is unusual in that it involves the simultaneous use of tequila and a wok.

1 1/2 POUNDS BEEF SKIRT, FLANK, OR ROUND
   STEAK, FAT TRIMMED
1/4 CUP TEQUILA
1/2 CUP LIME JUICE
1 CUP COOKING OIL
1 TABLESPOON LIQUID SMOKE
1 TEASPOON WORCESTERSHIRE SAUCE
1/4 TEASPOON PEPPER
1/2 TEASPOON SALT
3/4 TEASPOON PAPRIKA
1/2 CUP CHOPPED GREEN ONIONS, INCLUDING TOPS
3/4 CUP CHOPPED GREEN PEPPER
1 CUP CHOPPED TOMATOES
8 TO 10 6-INCH FLOUR OR CORN TORTILLAS

Slice the partially frozen beef steak into long strips, thinner than a pencil. Marinate 2 hours with a mixture of tequila and lime juice in a flat glass dish. Drain.

Combine oil, liquid smoke, Worcestershire sauce, pepper, salt, and paprika, beating with a rotary beater until smooth. Heat the wok over medium high heat, add the oil mixture, and swirl the wok in a circular motion. When hot, add the steak strips, stirring occasionally. Stir in the onion and green pepper 3 or 4 minutes before the steak is cooked. When done, ladle onto hot plates and top with chopped tomato. Wrap in warmed flour or corn tortillas.
Serves 4.

(1984 Texas Beef Cookoff second-place winner, Jean Conner, Palestine, Texas, and Texas Cowbelles Association)

THE GOOD OLD DAYS

There are those who would question there ever being a time that was actually "The Good Old Days!" They are quick to point out all the modern conveniences we have, especially in the food world. In this case I'm referring to "cold cuts," those handy packages of product that sometimes really contain a little meat. If properly handled, any real meat can be turned into very tasty lunch meats that make great sandwiches. Since the subject of this book is fajitas, I found a great way to prepare them a little differently.

3 POUNDS SKIRT STEAK (OR ANY OTHER "REAL" MEAT)

SALT

1 CLOVE GARLIC

1 BUNCH GREEN ONIONS

1 GREEN PEPPER

1/4 CUP MINCED PARSLEY

1 CUP OLIVE OIL

1/3 CUP RED WINE

SALT AND PEPPER

CUMIN

Slice skirt steaks as for fajitas. Simmer with salt and clove of garlic until meat is tender. Drain off water and let cool. Arrange in layers in the bottom of a fairly deep dish. Chop onions and green pepper and mix with parsley, olive oil, wine, salt, pepper, and cumin to taste. Pour this over the meat and let stand overnight in the fridge before serving. Serve cold on warm tortillas.

31

Great Alternatives

These recipes are for those who have tried the regular recipes and want to expand into the more esoteric ways of preparing fajitas. All involve using 2 to 3 pounds of skirt steaks; the primary differences are in the methods of preparation.

FAJITABURGERS

In 1987, Jack in the Box introduced the fajita pita—it is only a matter of time before Burger King, Wendy's, Taco Bell, and the others follow suit. So, before you are subjected to the McFajita, learn to make the real thing.

When making the fajitaburgers, follow the same rules as you would for regular hamburgers. Don't squeeze the burger patties together too tightly. Be careful with the spatula—don't compress. And, if grilling, add a bit of crushed ice to the patties. This keeps the burgers moist.

2 POUNDS SKIRT STEAK

EGG (OPTIONAL)

1/4 CUP BREADCRUMBS (OPTIONAL)

WORCESTERSHIRE SAUCE (OPTIONAL)

BLACK PEPPER (OPTIONAL)

VEGETABLE OIL

GUACAMOLE WITH CILANTRO

SAUTEED ONIONS

KAISER ROLL

CHEDDAR OR SWISS CHEESE

First, find a good heavy-duty meat grinder. Oster and Hamilton Beach models or Cuisinart on "chop" or "medium grind" work quite well.

Next, remove the fat and membrane from 2 pounds of fajitas and send them through the grinder—twice. Some purists suggest nothing else should be added to the meat, but it is often a good idea to add an egg and 1/4 cup breadcrumbs for consistency. Those who want more hamburger taste can include a dash of Worcestershire sauce and freshly ground black pepper. Avoid salt: It tends to make the patties much too dry.

Shape the patties into 10-ounce mounds about 2 inches thick. Fry briefly in hot vegetable oil, then transfer to the broiler section and heat at 350 to 400° F. Top with guacamole mixed with cilantro.

Serve open-faced with sautéed onions on a Kaiser roll with a slice of aged cheddar or Swiss cheese. Serves 5–8.

The nice thing about chopped meat burgers is that you can add all sorts of things to them: chopped onions, chopped or sliced mushrooms, parsley, cilantro, shallots, mustard, chives, cumin, tarragon, marjoram, paprika, thyme, or oregano.

FAJITA SUBMARINES

This recipe is for die-hard easterners who *must* have their submarine sandwich (poor boy, hoagie, etc.).

2 POUNDS SKIRT STEAK
1 16-OUNCE BOTTLE ITALIAN DRESSING
1–2 PATS BUTTER OR MARGARINE
1 ONION, COARSELY CHOPPED
PIMIENTO (OPTIONAL)
1 BELL PEPPER, SLICED
4 TO 6 SUBMARINE BUNS
MOZZARELLA CHEESE (OPTIONAL)
DRESSING OF CHOICE

First trim and tenderize the fajitas using the knife and fork method (see the chapter, "How to Trim a Fajita"). Marinate in Italian dressing for 24 hours in the refrigerator. Place in a covered plastic dish in the freezer compartment for 4 hours. Remove and slice the frozen meat with an electric knife. Brown in a Teflon pan with ⅛ cup water and a small amount of butter or margarine. Sauté onions, pimiento, and sliced bell pepper. Add to submarine or hoagie buns, with a few layers of mozzarella cheese and serve with your favorite dressing (horseradish, mustard, Italian dressing, mayo). Serves 4 to 6.

LITE FAJITAS

Those who are watching their weight might consider fajitas prepared with only lime juice and paprika. They seem to work well together with both chicken and beef. The fajitas are marinated in the lime juice, tenderized using the knife and fork method, then dusted with mild paprika. Grill under the oven broiler and finish off in a Teflon pan with ⅛ cup water instead of cooking oil.

CHICKEN-FRIED FAJITA *BOTANAS*

Those addicted to quiche and similar fare can first tenderize ¼-inch strips of fajitas using the knife and fork method, marinate in Campbell's cream of mushroom soup, then dip in egg batter. After that, the strips are rolled in flour and fried in vegetable oil. The result is a combination fajita/chicken-fried steak/*botana* taste.

Barbacoa and Cabrito

In the interest of fairness, this book includes a few of the alternatives to fajitas that have, on occasion, appeared on several South Texas menus. If you would believe owners and operators of the big Mexican restaurant chains, there are all sorts of dishes that rival fajitas: enchiladas, tamales, tacos *al carbón* (which are merely tacos with teeny, tiny chunks of fajitas in them), quesadillas, chimichangas, and a variety of other eats with Mexican-sounding names.

In truth, however, the rivals to fajitas as the best dish in South Texas number only two: *barbacoa de cabeza* and *cabrito al pastor*. These alternative edibles are considered, each in its appropriate setting.

There is a certain something about having a picnic on the beach, amid the wind, sand, gulls, and good friends. Fajitas, of course, are terrific when grilled on the beach, particularly if it's South Padre Island during spring break or a much-needed vacation: The night air is cold enough to require a warm jacket and/or snuggling with a friend. Additionally, you don't mind if the beer is ambient temperature, since that is usually down in the mid-fifties.

It is usually a good idea to bring your own grill and charcoal or firewood. If you *must* use driftwood, you should know that it seems to be more plentiful the farther up the Texas coast you go. While the beach near Corpus Christi and Aransas Pass always seems to contain adequate amounts, the beaches much closer to Port Isabel are usually bare. At least I've never seen much. I suspect it is scarfed up by the major hotels to be used for decorative purposes.

At any rate, if you happen to be on the beach at Padre in the spring, you may notice a barbecue of a slightly different nature: *cabeza eposo* (head in the hole), sometimes simply *barbacoa de cabeza*. While this doesn't involve fajitas, it is certainly worth mentioning, because it is the great-granddaddy of Mexican Gulf Coast barbecue.

BARBACOA DE CABEZA

Before you actually get the *cabeza* (beef head), understand that it won't look very nice — in fact, it will look pretty gruesome. Therefore, I suggest purchasing the thing the day you cook it.

Mustang Island (which is the northern segment of the Padre-Mustang pair) is a great place to fix *barbacoa*. In addition, on certain spring nights, the Gulf is invested with tiny phosphorescent plankton, providing the unusual and beautiful light show of luminous waves crashing onto a luminous beach.

In the Rio Grande Valley, *barbacoa de cabeza* is traditionally eaten on Sunday mornings.

1 *CABEZA*, PURCHASED AT MEAT MARKET
SEVERAL ONIONS
SEVERAL BUDS OF GARLIC
2 BUNCHES OF CILANTRO
ADEQUATE SUPPLY OF CORN OR FLOUR TORTILLAS

Clean the *cabeza*, removing eyes, ears, etc. Discard the tongue. Leaving it will impart an odd taste to the meat. Wrap the *cabeza* in a paper sack, along with onions, garlic, and cilantro. Wrap *that* in burlap.

Dig a hole 2 feet deep and build a driftwood fire in it. Wait until the fire goes to coals, then cover them with ashes, followed by the *cabeza*, then about 2 inches of dry dirt or sand. Fill up the hole. Add 6 to 8 inches of dirt or sand over it. Build a fire on top of the ground. Use slow-burning wood such as oak or mesquite.

Leave the *cabeza* in the hole 12 to 18 hours. For example, if you begin cooking it at 4:00 p.m., it should be ready by the next morning. Serve with tortillas. Serves one vanload.

If you want to try *barbacoa de cabeza* at home, try wrapping the *cabeza* in foil and baking it in an oven or over a charcoal grill. Using foil in place of the paper bag keeps the *cabeza* slightly moister while cooking.

▼▼▼▼▼▼▼▼▼▼▼▼▼▼▼▼▼▼▼▼▼▼▼▼▼▼▼▼▼▼

CABRITO AL PASTOR

Another alternative to fajitas is kid goat or, more correctly, *cabrito*. Those lucky enough to find their way to the Mexican border towns will only have to follow their noses to locate the best grilled *cabrito* in North America. Typically, the restaurateur helps the tourists find their way by displaying the grilling area behind an 8-foot by 20-foot picture window, usually facing the street. There you will see a huge bed of charcoal and several racks of meat.

If you're unable to make it over to Mexico, you might try grilling your own *cabrito*. But make a taste test first. There are any number of Mexican restaurants that serve *cabrito*, usually in tacos. The meat is usually described as "gamey," skinny, and tough—all accurate descriptions. Moreover, if the goat isn't prepared properly, you will find the meat has a thin coating of lanolin.

If, however, you decide to try it, here is the recipe, direct from Nuevo León and Tamaulipas and ready for the beach or your backyard grill.

2 *CABRITOS*, 7 TO 9 POUNDS EACH
1 TABLESPOON SALT
1 CUP WINE VINEGAR
2 QUARTS ITALIAN DRESSING

EXTRAS:
GUACAMOLE
4 TABLESPOONS WHITE ONION, CHOPPED
1 1/2 CUPS TOMATO, CHOPPED
1 CUP CILANTRO
2 TABLESPOONS CHILE PEPPERS (SERRANOS)
2 CUPS MONTEREY JACK CHEESE

While *cabrito al pastor* isn't quite as troublesome as *barbacoa de cabeza* to fix, it does have to be done right—otherwise the meat will either be too tough or have an unusual gamey taste.

While skinning the goats, remember that the hand that touches the hair never touches the meat. Try to use the left hand for the skin, the right hand for the knife. After skinning, wash the left hand—goat hair contains lanolin.

After cleaning, the *cabritos* should be placed in a large stock pot of water. Add the salt and wine vinegar. This is used to marinate the tough meat. Leave the *cabritos* in the stock pot for about 2 hours. While they are marinating, build a fire on the ground, preferably using mesquite, oak, or other slow-burning wood. Wait until the fire has been almost reduced to white coals, then remove the *cabritos* from the pot and baste with Italian dressing.

Thread the *cabritos* on spits and place over the coals, turning continuously to provide even cooking. The *cabritos* may be basted with salt water followed by Italian dressing.

Serve with guacamole or sprinkle with cheese. Serves 8.

THE BASICS: TASTY SIDE DISH RECIPES

TORTILLAS

It is conceivable that one could eat fajitas without tortillas, but one wonders why anyone would want to. Tortillas are soft and warm and people love them, especially with fajitas. Nowadays, no self-respecting restaurant would consider serving fajitas without them. That, however, was not always the case.

In 1972, for example, in the Rio Grande Valley there were only two restaurants serving reliable fajitas: the venerable Roundup in Pharr and its counterpart on the Mexican side, Los Portales, located on Calle Seis in rough, tough Matamoros. While both restaurants served wonderful corn and flour tortillas, it was considered somewhat gauche for the customer to plunk the steak into the tortilla, pour on the sauce, and roll the thing into a burrito. That was something that traveling musicians did to avoid airline food, not something to be done in an uptown restaurant. Back then, the idea was to savor the meat as is, like a fine steak; the tortilla, soaked in butter and dipped into the bean soup, was an added attraction.

Somehow, between 1972 and 1985, the fajita burrito was born, with customers rolling their own.

It is possible that this sort of thing came about as a throwback to the days when the ranch workers used tortillas as plates. It is possible that Mexican Americans, tired of defending the horrendous menudo, decided to adopt the fajita tortilla combo as the next fast food. Who knows?

I suspect, however, that the practice began on a Sunday morning, sometime in the mid-1970s, probably in or around one of the little string of Texas towns that hug the Rio Grande, with names like Weslaco, Donna, Mercedes, and Olmito.

There is a charming tradition in the Mexican neighborhoods that involves driving to the nearest market or restaurant immediately after church services and picking up a few pounds of *barbacoa de cabeza*, then stopping off at the nearest tortilla factory for some masa (corn) or harina (flour) tortillas. Anyone who has ever tried this wonderful food will find that it is both incredibly tasty and incredibly greasy. There is only one way to eat it: rolled inside a tortilla, preferably a *flour* tortilla. Corn tortillas are often too thin. If you happen to have a Sunday suit on, grease breakthrough can spell real trouble.

Anyway, I suspect that sooner or later someone really addicted to the *barbacoa*-tortilla combination put two and two together and tried it with fajitas. And while the 1940s Mexican ranch hand story has some merit, there were no tortilla factories around in those days and I suspect that the laborers were probably too busy to fix up a mess of tortillas just for one meal — tortillas take time.

The tortilla connection might have originated with straight barbecue. In the mid-1970s many inhabitants of the Rio Grande Valley, myself included, would spend weekends at the beach. And every weekend we would have a ritual: stop by either Mi Tierra or Bennie's Barbecue and pick up two pounds of meat along with seven or eight corn tortillas. Along with a six-pack of Pearl, it was the perfect beach food. If Bennie had offered fajitas (he didn't) I'm sure his customers would have wrapped the skirt steaks in tortillas and gone on their way.

But it may be that fajitas and tortillas always *did* go together, way back around the turn of the century, and the fast-food restaurants like Fajita Willie's, Fajitaville, and Two Pesos are just carrying on a long tradition.

HOW TO MAKE TORTILLAS

If you live in the Southwest, you're lucky — you don't have to make tortillas. Instead, you can drive to the nearest tortilla factory and buy any amount you need.

If, however, you live somewhere other than the Southwest, it's a different matter entirely. You may actually have to make the darn things. I assure you, it is not an easy task.

Flour tortillas are absolutely essential to the enjoyment of fajitas, so the method for their manufacture is provided in detail.

It should be noted that making tortillas is not so much a science as an art. The first few tries will probably result in one good tortilla against eleven others that are too thick, too fragile, lumpy, charred, or just plain inedible. Keep trying, though — the results are worth it. The ability to make a dozen perfect tortillas is a skill that ranks up there with gourmet cooking, juggling, and dancing the mashed potato — something that you'd almost want to put on your résumé.

MY OWN TORTILLAS

4 CUPS ALL PURPOSE FLOUR

1/4 CUP SHORTENING

SALT

DASH CAYENNE

1 CUP WATER

Cut shortening into flour; add salt, cayenne and water. Mix until a dough is formed, knead mixture shape into 2-inch balls. Roll out on a floured counter, board, or table. Makes 2 dozen 10-inch tortillas. Cook tortillas on hot griddle, preferably cast iron. No oil is necessary. Flip tortilla over just as it starts to puff.

FAJITA STEW

Tortillas don't always have to have something wrapped in them. Sometimes I like to eat them with a meal like I would bread. I even like them by themselves with nothing else. This is a little stew I found out about, and I think it's really good.

2 POUNDS SKIRT STEAK

2 TABLESPOONS BUTTER

1 MEDIUM ONION, FINELY CHOPPED

1/3 CUP CHOPPED GREEN PEPPER

3 CUPS CANNED CORN

10 1/2-OUNCE CAN TOMATO SOUP

2 TEASPOONS SUGAR

1 1/2 TEASPOON SALT

1 TABLESPOON WORCHESTERSHIRE SAUCE

Cut skirt steaks in narrow strips. Melt butter in heavy skillet. Add onion and green pepper. Cook until tender. Add meat and brown. Add corn, sugar, salt, and Worcestershire. Simmer for an hour. Serve in bowls with tortillas instead of bread.

A BRIEF HISTORY OF THE TORTILLA

CORN TORTILLAS ARE AS OLD AS THE MAYANS, PERHAPS EVEN OLDER. MAYAN LEGEND CLAIMS THAT THE GOD QUETZALCOATL INTRODUCED TORTILLAS TO THE FIRST MAN, OXOMOCO, AND WOMAN, CIPACTONAL. FLOUR TORTILLAS SHOWED UP A WHILE LATER, AROUND 1900 OR THEREABOUTS. LIKE FAJITAS, THEY ARE PRETTY MUCH A NORTHERN MEXICO PHENOMENON; HARINA TORTILLAS ARE AS DIFFICULT TO COME BY IN MEXICO CITY AS SKIRT STEAKS.

MASA TORTILLAS CAN VARY IN COLOR, DEPENDING UPON THE TYPE OF CORN USED. FOR EXAMPLE, IT IS POSSIBLE TO HAVE RED, BLUE, AND EVEN BLACK TORTILLAS, ALL PERFECTLY EDIBLE.

THE REGIONAL DIFFERENCES AMONG HARINA TORTILLAS USUALLY HAVE TO DO WITH SIZE. FLOUR TORTILLAS FOUND IN ARIZONA TEND TO BE LARGE, OFTEN 18 INCHES IN DIAMETER, WHILE THOSE FOUND IN CENTRAL AND WEST TEXAS ARE MORE MODERATELY SIZED, AT 7 INCHES.

IN THE MID-1970S, HOWEVER, IN THE RIO GRANDE VALLEY A TORTILLA WAR CULMINATED IN ONE RESTAURANT— HARLINGEN'S CUEVAS NO. 7—OFFERING A 24-INCH TORTILLA. IT WAS JUST THE THING AT 3 A.M. ON SUNDAY. WITH A BIT OF SALT AND A LOT OF BUTTER, A PERSON COULD SCRAPE AN ENTIRE EARLY BREAKFAST OF CHORIZO AND EGGS INTO THE WORLD'S BIGGEST BURRITO.

MASA TORTILLAS

Masa tortillas are not crucial to fajitas; the recipe is supplied for informational purposes only.

2 CUPS MASA HARINA (CORN FLOUR)
1 TEASPOON SALT
1 1/4 CUPS WATER

Mix the masa harina, salt, and water together to make the tortilla dough. Roll the dough into even balls about the size of Ping-Pong balls. Place a sheet of wax paper on the bottom of a tortilla press. Put the masa ball on top of the wax paper and cover it with another sheet of wax paper. Press down the tortilla press. Open it and peel off the wax paper from the top and bottom of the flattened tortilla. If the tortilla splits around the edges, or is dry and crumbly, add a little more water to the dough. If the tortilla sticks to the press, add a little more masa harina to the dough.

If you do not own a tortilla press you can prepare corn tortillas the way it is traditionally done in Mexico. Place one of the masa balls into the palm of your hand and press the ball from side to side in your palm until the tortilla is flat and smooth (about 3½ inches in diameter).

Tortillas are usually cooked on a *comal*, an iron or unglazed earthenware griddle. If you do not have a *comal*, a large skillet is just as effective. Place the flattened tortillas on the *comal* or skillet until the edges begin to dry (about ½ minute). Using a spatula, quickly flip the tortilla over. Since the opposite side is already hard, this side should puff up slightly when done. Remove the cooked tortillas to a cloth-covered bowl. Makes 12 to 18 tortillas.

WHEAT FLOUR TORTILLAS

4 CUPS WHEAT FLOUR

1 1/2 TEASPOONS SALT

1/2 CUP SHORTENING

1 CUP WATER

Sift the flour and salt together and cut in the shortening. Stir in the water with a fork until a sticky dough forms. Remove the dough from the bowl and knead it on a lightly floured surface until smooth. Return the dough to the bowl, cover it, and let it rest in a draft-free area for 1½ hours. Divide the dough into Ping-Pong–size balls; on a lightly floured surface, roll out the dough into a thin, even circle like a piecrust. Cook the dough on a hot *comal* or griddle for about ½ minute on each side. Remove the cooked tortillas to a cloth-covered bowl. Makes 12 to 18 tortillas. To reheat tortillas, wrap them in a dampened paper towel, place them in a microwave oven, and heat on high for 1 minute.

BEANS

Fajitas and beans are a great food combination. Beans are a versatile, inexpensive, and filling side dish to serve at your next fajita cookout.

To prepare the beans, rinse and sort them. Look carefully for rocks, twigs, and other foreign matter. Discard any discolored beans. Place the beans and water in a Dutch oven or kettle and bring them to a rapid boil. Remove the beans from the heat, cover, and let stand 1 hour.

Beans can also be cleaned and then soaked for 8 hours or overnight with enough water to cover. Drain and add 4 quarts of fresh water. Cook as directed in the recipes. Dried beans swell to double or more their original bulk as they cook.

ANN'S BASIC BEANS

2 CUPS DRIED PINK, RED, OR BLACK BEANS

8 CUPS WATER

1 MEDIUM ONION, CHOPPED

2 TEASPOONS GARLIC POWDER

1/2 TEASPOON SALT

OPTIONAL:

1 SMALL HAM HOCK, 1 HAM BONE, 2 OR 3 SLICES OF BACON, 2 SLICES OF SALT PORK, OR 1 TABLESPOON BACON FAT

Prepare the beans as directed above. Cook the beans on medium to low heat with the ham hock, ham bone, bacon, or salt pork and the onion and garlic powder for 1½ hours or until tender. Do not add salt to the beans until their skins wrinkle and burst or they will toughen. Keep the beans covered with water, adding hot water as needed. Serves 8.

MEXICALI BEANS

2 CUPS PINTO BEANS

8 CUPS WATER

3 SLICES BACON, DICED, OR 1 TABLESPOON
  BACON FAT

3 GREEN CHILI PEPPERS, SEEDED AND DICED

2 CLOVES GARLIC, DICED

1 ONION, DICED

1 SMALL CAN TOMATOES

2 TEASPOONS SALT

Clean and prepare the beans as above. Cook the bacon until it is almost done. Add the chile peppers, garlic, and onion to the bacon and cook until lightly browned. Then add the chili peppers, garlic, onion, bacon, and tomatoes to the beans and cook on medium to low heat for 1½ hours until the beans are tender. Do not add salt to the beans until their skins wrinkle or burst. Keep beans covered with water, adding hot water as needed. Serves 8.

REFRIED BEANS

2 CUPS COOKED BEANS

1/2 CUP SHORTENING OR BACON DRIPPINGS

1 TEASPOON SALT

1 TEASPOON OREGANO

Mash the cooked beans with a potato masher. Heat the shortening or bacon drippings in a pan and add the mashed beans, salt, and oregano. Cook until all the shortening or bacon drippings have been absorbed, stirring constantly to prevent the beans from sticking. Serves 8. Variations: Add cubed Monterey Jack or cheddar cheese; top with sour cream and mild green chiles; or sprinkle the beans with pieces of cooked bacon and diced green onions.

RICE

Although there are many different recipes for rice, I've chosen three that go well with fajitas and are easy to prepare. You may substitute commercial precooked rice in any of these recipes. Cook the rice as directed on the package.

If you have rice left over from another meal, it can be reheated and used in the Spicy Rice and Quick 'N' Easy Rice recipes. To reheat rice, use ¼ cup water for each cup of cooked rice (stored in the refrigerator). Put the water and cold cooked rice in a saucepan, breaking up any clumps. Place saucepan on high heat. When the water around the edges of the saucepan begins to bubble, place a lid on the saucepan and turn the heat as low as possible to heat thoroughly. Turn off the heat and leave the lid on until the rice is ready to be served.

SPICY RICE

1 CUP UNCOOKED WHITE RICE

2 CUPS WATER

1 TEASPOON SALT

3 SLICES OF BACON, DICED

2 TABLESPOONS ONION, DICED

2 TABLESPOONS GREEN PEPPER, DICED

1 CUP TOMATO JUICE

1/4 TEASPOON PEPPER

1/4 TEASPOON CUMIN

1 TEASPOON CHILI POWDER

Combine the rice, water, and salt in a 2-quart saucepan and bring to a vigorous boil. Turn the heat down to low. Cover the saucepan with a lid and cook for 15 minutes. Do not remove the lid while the rice is cooking. Then remove the rice from the heat and set aside, covered. Cook the bacon until crisp in a frying pan, then set aside. Cook the onion and green pepper in the bacon fat until golden brown and tender.

Add tomato juice, pepper, cumin, chili powder, and bacon to the cooked rice. Simmer 10 minutes, or until most of tomato juice has been absorbed by the rice, stirring occasionally to prevent sticking. Serves 6.

GREEN RICE

2 CUPS WHITE RICE

1 CAN SERRANO CHILIS OR 2 FRESH CHILIS, SEEDED AND DICED

2 CLOVES GARLIC

2 SPRIGS CILANTRO

3 BELL PEPPERS, SEEDED AND DICED

1 ONION

1/4 CUP OIL

1/4 CUP PARSLEY

1 TEASPOON SALT

2 CANS CHICKEN BROTH

Soak the rice in a bowl of hot water for 15 minutes. Rinse the rice thoroughly with cold water, then drain well and set aside. In a blender, puree the chiles, garlic, cilantro, bell peppers, onion, and parsley. Heat the oil in a Dutch oven and fry the rice until it is golden brown. Add the puree and salt to the rice and cook the mixture for 5 minutes. Pour the broth over the rice. Cover and steam the rice for 20 minutes over low heat until the broth is absorbed and the rice is done. Serves 6.

QUICK 'N' EASY RICE

2 CUPS COOKED RICE
2 TABLESPOONS BUTTER
1 TABLESPOON CHILI POWDER
1/4 TEASPOON CUMIN

Toss the cooked rice lightly with butter, chili powder, and cumin. Serves 4.

SYNTHETIC GUAC

IF THE PARTY'S JUST AN HOUR AWAY AND YOU HAVE ABSOLUTELY NO TIME WHATSOEVER, THEN PUT A FEW DOLLARS IN YOUR POCKET, GO TO THE STORE, AND BUY SOME AVOCADOS AND "AVO-CADO HELPER." THIS STUFF GOES BY A VARIETY OF NAMES, BUT IT USUALLY COMES IN A FLAT PACKAGE, COSTS LESS THAN A DOLLAR, AND OFFERS A VARIETY OF TASTES, FROM "MILD" TO "EXTRA SPICY." TYPICALLY, ALL THE CHEF HAS TO DO IS MASH TWO AVOCADOS, POUR IN A PACKET OF THE "HELPER," MIX IT UP, AND REFRIGERATE IT ABOUT 30 MINUTES.

IN EXCHANGE FOR YOUR TIME, YOUR GUACAMOLE WILL CONTAIN MALTO DEX-TRIN, SALT, DEHYDRATED ONION, NONFAT DRY MILK, RED BELL PEPPER, AVOCADO POWDER, MODIFIED TAPIOCA STARCH, SOUR CREAM POWDER, GROUND JALA-PENOS, LEMON JUICE POWDER, GREEN CHIVES, ASCORBIC ACID, CRUSHED RED PEPPERS, AND CITRIC ACID.

IT'S GOOD, BUT IS IT GUACAMOLE?

DEPENDS ON YOUR TASTE. AS ANY GUA-CAMOLE ADDICT WILL TELL YOU: EVEN WHEN GUACAMOLE IS BAD, IT'S STILL GOOD.

GUACAMOLE

Back in the 1930s, fruit growers in Florida and the Southwest were speculating on the possibilities of a strange, bland-tasting critter they called an "alligator pear." Its chances, they decided, weren't too good. For one thing, it was usually hard as a rock. It was also difficult to peel. And, despite its name, it tasted nothing like a real pear. It was one of many fruits and vegetables that had been cultivated by the Indians for centuries, but in spite of its long heritage the alligator pear seemed destined for flat-out rejection.

Then someone suggested calling it by its Spanish name: avocado. Maybe the same person decided to use avocado in recipes similar to the ones the Indians had used for centuries, right down to the lime juice, tomatoes, and peppers.

Thus guacamole was introduced to a discerning public.

Most of us first became acquainted with guacamole in high school or college, while squeezed into one of the impossibly narrow chairs that are so common at Mexican restaurants. Or maybe you first found it at that party, the one where the girl with the cutoff jeans brought that whole bowl of green stuff and claimed it was some sort of dip.

No matter—one taste of "guac" usually hooks most people forever on the subtle yet spicy flavor. I have known people who refuse to show up at a party unless guacamole is also in attendance. I am acquainted with people who grade Mexican restaurants on the quality of their avocado dip. I know people who swear that they will eat in the worst Mexican restaurant in town if it serves free guac with the tostadas. That, of course, will never happen.

For those readers of the northern persuasion, an important fact: in the Southwest, the tostadas or fried masa tortilla chips are usually free of charge. That's right. One might even get the salsa for free, but guacamole? *Lo siento*, señor—guacamole you pay for.

Perhaps it *is* a lot of trouble to mash the avocados up, add a bit of chopped tomatoes, a little lime juice, and a bit of jalapeño. I suspect, however, the real reason that guacamole is not free is that people become addicted to guacamole just as they become addicted to Pepsi and Pringle's. There's something there, hidden deep in either the taste or the texture, or both, that demands you scrape the bottom of the guacamole dish at the party until it's dishwasher clean.

If you're a true fajita fan, you probably demand only the best guacamole—so you should probably make it yourself.

Start with avocados that are *slightly soft* to the touch. Supermarkets often "push ripen" fruit using a variety of chemicals, none of which are particularly conducive to taste. Therefore, the best place to purchase avocados is probably at the local farmer's market.

You won't have to poke or plonk the avocado like a watermelon to determine if it is suffi-

ciently ripe. Rather, squeeze the entire avocado gently. If it yields to slight pressure, it's okay. Often all the grocer has are underripe avocados. If that's the case, buy some of the better-looking ones and throw them into a paper bag. Leave them at room temperature (70° F) for a few days, and they will ripen up just fine.

BASIC GUACAMOLE

Though mashed avocado by itself is pretty bland fare, only the lemon/lime juice is really essential. Without it, the guac turns a surly brown and just sits there looking bad.

2 RIPE AVOCADOS

DASH OF ONION JUICE

1/2 TABLESPOON LIME JUICE

1/2 TABLESPOON LEMON JUICE

1 SMALL TOMATO, SEEDED AND CHOPPED

2 SCALLIONS, CHOPPED

3/4 GREEN PEPPER, SEEDED AND CHOPPED

1 TEASPOON OLIVE OR COTTONSEED OIL

1/2 TEASPOON CILANTRO LEAVES, CHOPPED

OPTIONAL:

1/2 TEASPOON PEPPER OF CHOICE (VARIABLE)

2 ARTICHOKE HEARTS IN COTTONSEED OIL, CHOPPED

1/2 TEASPOON HORSERADISH

1/2 TEASPOON SHALLOTS, CHOPPED

DASH OF MINCED GARLIC

CILANTRO

First, peel the avocados and mash with a fork. Good guacamole should have a few lumps of real avocado mixed in with the other ingredients. Food processors are acceptable avocado-mashing instruments, but blenders do the job *too* well, turning the avocados to mush or, worse, to liquid.

Add the remaining ingredients, then add any or all of the optional ingredients, a small amount at a time, until you arrive at a taste you like. Sprinkle the surface of the guacamole with cilantro, if desired. Serves 2.

SALADS

Surveys indicate that fajitas seem to taste best when grilled out-of-doors, particularly in the springtime along the banks of almost any Texas river. It may only be a coincidence, but salads seem to taste best under similar conditions. So if your group plans a fajita cookout and it's your turn to bring the greens, you're in luck: here are a few salad recipes that seem to work well.

CHICKPEA SALAD

1 14-OUNCE CAN CHICKPEAS

3 GREEN ONIONS, MINCED

2 STALKS CELERY, MINCED

1/2 SMALL BELL PEPPER, MINCED

2 TABLESPOONS WINE VINEGAR

2 TABLESPOONS OLIVE OIL

Rinse the chickpeas in cold water. Combine all the ingredients and refrigerate overnight. Serves 4.

CHEF SALAD

DRESSING:

1/4 CUP EACH WINE VINEGAR AND MAYONNAISE

3/4 CUP VEGETABLE OIL (WITH SLIGHT AMOUNT
OF COTTONSEED OR OLIVE OIL)

1 CLOVE GARLIC, CRUSHED

SALT AND PEPPER

8 CUPS GREENS, TORN OR CUT INTO BITE-SIZED
PIECES (USE ICEBERG, BOSTON OR BUTTER
LETTUCE, ROMAINE, AND SPINACH LEAVES)

1/4 POUND COOKED, SHELLED SHRIMP, HALVED

1/4 POUND SMOKED TURKEY, SLIVERED

1/4 POUND BAKED HAM, SLIVERED

1/4 POUND FETA CHEESE IN 1/2-INCH CUBES

1/8 POUND SWEDISH FARMER'S CHEESE IN
1/2-INCH CUBES

1/8 POUND MONTEREY JACK CHEESE IN 1/2-INCH
CUBES

2 LARGE TOMATOES, SLICED, OR 12 CHERRY
TOMATOES

GARNISH: 4 TO 6 SLICES CRUMBLED CRISP BACON
OR CHERRY PEPPERS

Combine all the ingredients and mix well.
Serves 8 to 10.

(Adapted from Emmanuel Greenberg, "Getting
It on with Greens," *Playboy*, August 1980,
p. 151)

VINAIGRETTE SALAD DRESSING

1 EGG YOLK

1 TEASPOON DIJON MUSTARD

1/4 CUP RED WINE VINEGAR

1 TABLESPOON PARSLEY, CHOPPED

1 CUP VEGETABLE OIL (PART OLIVE OIL OR
COTTONSEED OIL)

Admittedly, this dressing tastes best with salad
as the main course, but if the reason for the
meal is the fajitas, this will do just fine.

Combine the ingredients except the oil in a
large bowl; whisk together until thickened.
Gradually add oil, while continuing to whisk.
Makes about 1½ cups.

(Adapted from Emmanuel Greenberg, "Getting
It on with Greens," *Playboy*, August 1980,
p. 151)

VINEGAR DRESSING

1/2 CUP VINEGAR

1/2 CUP SALAD OIL

1 CUP SUGAR

1/2 CUP CHOPPED ONION

1 TEASPOON PAPRIKA

1 TEASPOON DRY MUSTARD

1/2 TEASPOON CELERY SEED

1 TEASPOON SALT

4 OUNCES TOMATO SAUCE

Blend ingredients in blender, chill before serving.
This dressing will keep for weeks in the refrigerator.

NOPALITOS

Nopales are one of the oldest items of Mexican cuisine, predating even the Spanish conquest. For thousands of years, Indians had dined on the nopales in the spring, when they tasted best. After the Spanish arrived, the conquistadors began eating the cactus pads in connection with the Lenten tradition of meatless meals.

Nopales cut into strips and marinated in oil are commonly called nopalitos (little nopales) and can be easily purchased almost anywhere in Texas and elsewhere in specialty markets. The taste resembles okra. However, jalapeño peppers are often added to the mix, heating up the combination considerably.

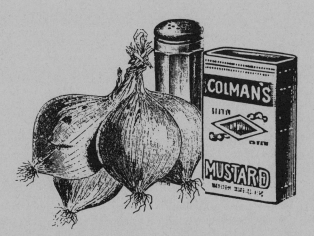

FONDA SAN MIGUEL NOPALITOS SALAD

1 16-OUNCE JAR NOPALITOS OR 2 CUPS STRIPS OF
    COOKED FRESH NOPALES (ABOUT 3 LEAVES),
    RINSED WELL
3 TABLESPOONS OLIVE OIL
4 TABLESPOONS RED WINE VINEGAR
1/2 TEASPOON LEAF OREGANO
2 TOMATOES, PEELED AND CHOPPED (1 CUP), WELL-
    DRAINED
1/2 WHITE ONION, CHOPPED
1 SMALL BUNCH CILANTRO, CHOPPED
DASH OF BLACK PEPPER
RED TIP LETTUCE
1 PICKLED JALAPENO OR SERRANO CHILE, SEEDED,
    STEM REMOVED, AND SLICED
FETA CHEESE (OR TEXAS GOAT CHEESE), CRUMBLED
WEDGES OF WHITE MEXICAN CHEESE
    (FARMER'S CHEESE WORKS WELL) OR MONTEREY
    JACK
AVOCADO AND TOMATO WEDGES

Make sure the nopales have had their stickers removed. If not, remove them carefully using gloves. There is nothing worse than biting down on a cactus needle. Cook in boiling, slightly salted water until the color changes to a dull green. Drain and cool. Rinse under cool water until no longer sticky. Pat dry and cut in strips. Combine the olive oil, red wine vinegar, oregano, tomatoes, onion, cilantro, and pepper. Toss lightly with the cactus strips and marinate at least an hour, preferably overnight.

Arrange on red tip or leaf lettuce. Garnish with 1 or 2 pieces of jalapeño, a little crumbled feta cheese, and wedges of white cheese, avocado, and tomato. Serves 4 to 6.

This particular salad, made from nopalitos, is nothing short of extraordinary and probably should be considered the main meal.

(Adapted from the Fonda San Miguel Restaurant in Austin; reported in the *Houston Chronicle*, January 14, 1987)

DRINKS

While either grilling or consuming fajitas, people have been known to drink all sorts of things, from water to tequila. Since both fajitas and tequila margaritas are normally found at Mexican restaurants, the general public (at least in the Southwest) has sort of assumed they go together. Actually, there are a lot of fine drinks that fall somewhere between Evian bottled water and José Cuervo Centenario.

AN ASIDE: MEZCAL

Those venturing into Mexican liquor stores may find, in addition to the various brands of tequila, a strange bottle with a cartoon of a red worm on it. The brand name emblazoned across the top will be something like Gusano Rojo (red worm). The customer will perhaps note that something is lying at the bottom of the bottle, looking suspiciously like a creepy little white worm. That is because it *is* a creepy little white worm.

And the drink inside the bottle is not tequila, but its backwoods cousin, mezcal.

Mezcal enjoys some popularity among the inhabitants of Matamoros and Reynosa: the Mexicans don't drink it, but they enjoy seeing the *gabachos* spend their hard-earned cash on a drink that tastes like fuel oil. They know there are few things worse than waking up after a night of revelry and drink and noticing an empty bottle of Gusano Rojo lying on the floor—with no worm inside.

It is the Mexican revenge for the annexation of Texas.

BASIC MARGARITAS

Margaritas are made from tequila, which is in turn made from Mexican agave plant (not a cactus) grown in the Sierra Madre near — where else? — the town of Tequila.

The agave resembles a 2½-foot-tall pineapple plant. When mature — after about ten years' growth — the plant is cut and the pulp actually *baked* for about 24 hours. After the baking process, the pulp is crushed and the sap, called *aguamiel* (honey water), is recovered. The *aguamiel* is then fermented, distilled, and occasionally aged in wooden casks. The resulting liquid may vary considerably in color, based upon the amount of aging involved. Clear tequila is aged the least amount of time, while the dark varieties such as Anejo or Cuervo's Centenario are aged much longer. Usually the clear or "golden" tequilas prove quite tasty in margaritas, while the Centenario varieties have a smokier taste similar to Scotch — and heaven knows you wouldn't want to add lime juice, ice, and salt to Scotch. Here is the basic all-purpose margarita recipe. It can be rendered to an acceptable slush by tossing it into the blender, along with a few ice cubes.

6 OUNCES TEQUILA (PREFERABLY JOSE CUERVO ANEJO)

3 OUNCES TRIPLE SEC (AN ORANGE-FLAVORED LIQUEUR)

1 TEASPOON LIME JUICE

5 MEDIUM-SIZED ICE CUBES (PREFERABLY FROM BOTTLED WATER)

JUICE OF 1/2 LIME

1 SMALL DISH MORTON'S KOSHER SALT

Mix the tequila, Triple Sec, and 1 teaspoon lime juice with the ice in a blender. Moisten the rim of a cocktail glass with lime juice, then dip the rim in Morton's kosher salt. Garnish with lime rind. Serves 1.

Some bartenders suggest adding a raw egg to the recipe; it makes the resultant drink somewhat smoother.

FROZEN MARGARITAS

If you find yourself in a fajita restaurant requiring a margarita, you might ask for the frozen variety. Specially designed cooling units take the drink to 28° F, turning it to slush.

A word of caution, however: cold drinks are a little bit more difficult to taste (why do you think purveyors of extremely cheap wine suggest serving their product very chilled?); therefore, you may not be able to gauge the alcohol level adequately. In other words, frozen margaritas can sneak up on you.

Not only that—they also can dry you out. If the restaurant is kind enough to rim the glass with salt, then two margaritas with no water on the side will practically guarantee you a headache the next morning. A suggestion: with each margarita you order, drink a glass of water.

Replicating the restaurant's margaritas is a chancy proposition. For one thing, the margarita-freezer is one expensive piece of equipment.

1 CUP WHITE OR GOLD TEQUILA
1 6-OUNCE CAN FROZEN LIMEADE CONCENTRATE
1/2 CUP TRIPLE SEC OR COINTREAU
3 TO 4 CUPS ICE CUBES
LIME WEDGE

Combine the tequila, limeade concentrate, and Triple Sec in a blender, then add ice cubes one by one until slushy. Serves 8.

TEQUILA SUNRISE

In the mid-1970s there was a popular drink called the tequila sunrise. It had actually been around for quite some time; the bartenders in Reynosa and Matamoros called it a tequila *madrugada* (tequila dawn). By the late-1980s the tequila sunrise seemed to have diminished in popularity somewhat. However, those who still own all of the Doobie Brothers albums and can name all the members of Deep Purple are probably the same ones who will clamor for a sunrise at your next barbecue.

It should be noted that there is also something called a tequila sunset. It is made the same way as a sunrise, except that blackberry or raspberry brandy is used in place of grenadine or maraschino cherry juice.

1 OUNCE CLEAR TEQUILA
ORANGE JUICE
1/2 OUNCE GRENADINE OR MARASCHINO CHERRY JUICE
MARASCHINO CHERRY GARNISH

Pour the tequila in a glass and add orange juice until it is nearly full. Then s-l-o-w-l-y add the grenadine so that it sinks to the bottom. If you substitute maraschino cherry juice, you will get a pink sunrise that's not really a sunrise, one that's slightly overcast—very similar, in fact, to an actual sunrise at Padre Island. Serves 1.

SANGRIA

Bars in Reynosa are noted for several things—among them, Harvey Wallbangers and an especially deadly form of sangría. While Harvey Wallbangers are just the thing to drink while trying to dance on the tables at the Club Imperial or La Siberia, sangría seems to work better on a hot Texas evening.

Sangría is the ultimate light alcoholic drink, a mixture of wine and soda water, sometimes spiked with harmless amounts of brandy just to give it an edge. It is unquestionably the predecessor of the ubiquitous "wine coolers" that now flood the market. So, rather than grabbing for that commercially prepared bottle of Tahiti-Guava-Wine-Punch-Cooler, try fixing up the real thing.

1/2 TO 3/4 CUP SUGAR OR SIMPLE SYRUP

1/2 CUP WATER

1 LEMON, CUT INTO THIN ROUND SLICES

1 LIME, CUT INTO THIN ROUND SLICES

1 ORANGE, CUT INTO THIN ROUND SLICES

1 LITER DRY RED WINE (BURGUNDY IS PERFECT)

2 8-OUNCE GLASSES OF SPARKLING WATER (CLUB SODA WITHOUT SALT, PERRIER, ETC.)

2 TABLESPOONS BRANDY OF CHOICE

1/2 CUP SWEET DARK CHERRIES

ICE CUBES

Combine the sugar or simple syrup and water in a saucepan, along with the end slices from the lemon, lime, and orange. Constantly stir and heat until boiling or until sugar dissolves. At this point you have fruit cooked in sugar syrup. Let cool and then squeeze the cooked fruit to add more juice to the syrup. Throw away the cooked fruit.

Combine the syrup, wine, sparkling water, brandy, fruit slices, and cherries in a large pitcher. Pour into ice-filled wine glasses. Serves 12.

MEXICAN BEERS

There are any number of beers that go well with fajitas—and most of them are made in Mexico. Many fajita restaurants serve any or all of the following Mexican brews: Corona, Tecate, Dos Equis, Bohemia, Superior, Carta Blanca.

Corona Extra: probably the brand in Texas that goes best with fajitas. Light and dry, it works best when the bottles are stored in an iced galvanized tub, as at Houston's Fajita Willie's. Back in 1977 you usually couldn't find this beer in Texas—had to go to Matamoros to get it. Somehow or other, the South Texas advertising gurus discovered the beer; ten years later you could see T-shirts and sweats sporting the Corona label. It's the perfect beer to go with fajitas.

Tecate: a beer that almost every college kid, at one time or another, has tried—with a lime. I suspect the lime bit was added by some ad man as a joke or perhaps to mask the strange metallic taste associated with the brew. Lime juice with beer tastes terrible, almost as bad as it does with fajitas. This beer stayed south of the border for years, then suddenly found its way to (of all places) Chicago sometime around 1978. At least, that's when I first saw the billboards for it. Oddly, you still couldn't buy it in Houston then.

Dos Equis: first wrested the limelight from Corona Extra in the mid-1970s. It is a somewhat heavier brew than Corona.

Bohemia: a lot of beer connoisseurs who normally would drink only Czech beer (e.g., Pilsner Urquell) have been fooled into ordering Bohemia. Sure, there is only one Bohemia, and it's in Central Europe. Sure, there is no place even remotely resembling Bohemia south of the Texas-Mexico border. Sure, this is a great beer.

Superior: a good beer to drink while having fajitas—or just about anything else. It is the Mexican equivalent of Budweiser.

Carta Blanca: remembered by South Texans for its unusual bottle. During the early 1970s the bottle had an indentation at the bottom—it was a bottle opener. All you had to do was stick the cap of the unopened bottle into the indentation, twist, and voila!—you had an open bottle of beer. The only thing was, in order to make it work, you had to buy *two* bottles. A few years later Carta Blanca realized it was a silly design and phased it out in favor of twist-off caps. It goes best with approximately a ton of chips.

AMERICAN BEERS THAT ARE ALMOST PERFECT WITH FAJITAS

There are only three: Pearl, Lone Star, and the legendary Shiner.

Pearl: made in San Antonio and a favorite in that city for years and years. Newcomers to San Antonio via the army or air force had a habit of stashing huge quantities in luggage during leave. As a result, places as far away as Boston learned that Pearl was as tasty as any snooty uptown brew.

Lone Star: the beer that won over college students on vacation at Padre Island.

Shiner: made in (where else?) Shiner, probably the best beer in Texas—for barbecue. It has a bit of a metallic taste (much like Tecate) that doesn't seem to go well with anything else. But, then again, it's better than most of the other American beers available—with the possible exception of the following.

LOCAL BEERS THAT WOULD GO GREAT WITH FAJITAS

While fajitas seem to go best with the Mexican imports (or San Antonio's Pearl and Shiner's Shiner), there are some other great beers from around the country that should also be considered:

	BEER	WHERE IT'S FOUND
1.	HENRY WEINHARD'S PRIVATE RESERVE	NATIONWIDE
2.	D. G. YUENGLING AND SON PILSNER	PENNSYLVANIA
3.	POINT SPECIAL	WISCONSIN
4.	IRON CITY	PENNSYLVANIA
5.	COLD SPRING EXPORT	MINNESOTA
6.	ROLLING ROCK	NATIONWIDE
7.	STROH'S	NATIONWIDE
8.	SAMUEL ADAMS	NATIONWIDE

FAJITAS AND MARGARITAS

First off, the two just seem to go together: fajitas and margaritas. It beats fajitas and piña coladas, fajitas and gin and tonics, fajitas and Tom Collins (the last sounds like the new married couple down the block). Perhaps this is the reason why fajitas caught on in Houston and Dallas (where margaritas are the number one bar drink) and not in Miami, Baltimore, and Los Angeles, where piña coladas, gin and tonics, and Tom Collins are preferred.

Here are the favorite drinks of various cities, along with a rating of how well that drink would go down with a fajita, guacamole, and tortilla.

CITY	DRINK	RATING
Houston	Margarita	Perfect
Dallas	Margarita	Perfect
New York	Long Island Iced Tea	On the right track
Los Angeles	Tom Collins	Has possibilities
Miami	Piña Colada	Has possibilities
Baltimore	Gin and tonic	Has possibilities
Portland, Oregon	Bourbon and water	Just maybe
Boston	Cape Cod	Doubtful
Chicago	Scotch and soda	Hold the Scotch
Pittsburgh	Whiskey, straight or on the rocks	Doubtful
San Diego	Rum and fruit juice	Doubtful
Seattle	Scotch on the rocks	Doubtful
Washington, D.C.	Vodka martini	Doubtful
Denver	Kahlua and coffee	Are you kidding?

(Source: Distilled Spirits Council)

A QUICK GUIDE TO TEX-MEX

It's been said that if you take two deep breaths, you will inhale at least three atoms of nitrogen that have also been inhaled by every man, woman, child, cat, dog, dinosaur, etc., that ever lived.

Similarly, if you survey every man, woman, and child in the United States and ask them to give an example of Mexican food, they will reply: "Tacos."

In fact, in the minds of most *norteamericanos*, Mexican food means tacos, taquitos, quesadillas, burritos, enchiladas, tostadas, and tamales. Some northerners even consider *chili* Mexican.

Well, fine, but if you really want Mexican food, ask for *pollo pibil, huachinango a la Veracruzana*, or even ceviche. Now *that's* Mexican. As for tacos, enchiladas, and the like, the sources of these dishes go all the way back to pre-Aztec civilizations on both sides of the Rio Grande, long before the Spanish conquistadors came along.

As for modern chili—well, it is a direct descendant of the chili con carne made by mission nuns in Mexico, who used beans, chopped meat, and a variety of chili peppers.

The dish similar to modern chili was invented by a German immigrant from New Braunfels who figured out a way to extract the pulp from chili pods. The pulp was then mixed with other spices and added to meat for chili con carne. The date: 1902, about the same time grilled fajitas were being "discovered" in the small towns along the Rio Grande.

Most fajita restaurants serve a variety of these foods. Here is a brief introduction to the fare you are likely to encounter.

ENCHILADA:

A food older than Mexico and probably older than the Aztecs. Typically consists of beef, chicken, or chorizo (pork sausage) wrapped in a corn or flour tortilla and covered with cheese. The Mexican varieties are somewhat spicier than the American versions.

TAMALE:

Masa (corn) dough surrounding beef or chicken and wrapped in a corn husk. Tamales are extremely popular all along the border and as far north as Canada. The husk surrounding the masa, of course, is *not* eaten; to do so is to risk great embarrassment and derisive laughter. Unfortunately, this little bit of information is usually left up to tourists to discover for themselves. It happened to Gerald Ford—it can happen to you.

TORTILLA:

A flat, round disk of unleaven bread. It can be made from either corn or wheat flour. Along the border, tourists from the North strive to impress the populace by asking for masa tortillas rather than the tastier wheat flour variety. Masa may not taste as good, but it certainly has more soul.

TACO:

Merely a tortilla filled with, well, anything and folded over. There are soft tacos, crispy tacos, tacos that shatter when you pick them up, tacos that break your teeth when you bite them, tacos that spill things on you, tacos that soak through and spill their contents in your lap, tacos of all shapes and sizes and price ranges.

Tacos represent the vanguard of the Tex-Mex invasion, the ground troops that paved the way for more esoteric (and mundane) kin: burritos, taquitos, quesadillas, and chimichangas (whatever they are). While tacos were popular on the West Coast in the late 1950s, the idea never really caught on until about 1962, when the ubiquitous Taco Bell first opened its doors in southern California. Tacos generally appeared in the Midwest about six years later, when teenage girls in Kansas City and St. Louis threw parties and served up huge corn tortillas dipped in vegetable oil and filled with lettuce, cheese, and hamburger.

TAQUITO:

A lesson in Spanish—add *-ito* to any Spanish noun and you get the diminutive, usually a term of endearment. A taquito, therefore, is really nothing more than a little taco. In 1986 Whataburger offered them as an entry in the Breakfast Wars. Pitted against a wide variety of breakfast croissants and bacon-egg-and-cheeses, the taquito did quite well.

TOSTADA:

A flat, crispy corn tortilla usually covered with fried beans and shredded lettuce. Occasionally one might find chorizo, beef, chicken, sour cream, or even guacamole. The interesting thing about the tostada is that it is difficult to eat gracefully. *Norteños* have been known to try to eat the thing like a sandwich, usually with hilarious results. For one thing, the shredded lettuce always falls off, taking everything with it. For another, the tostada always cracks at the first bite, usually right down the middle, or splinters into several very crispy masa fractals, dumping lettuce and guacamole into the customer's lap. Experienced tostada gourmets always ask for a fork.

FRIJOLES REFRITOS:

Pinto beans that have been simmered until they are soft, after which they are mashed and fried in vegetable oil. They may look starchy, but actually contain quite a few vitamins—and calories. Refritos, along with Spanish rice, constitute the bulk of the Tex-Mex restaurant trade.

QUESADILLA:

Originally this meant cheesecake. Mexican restaurants have extended the term to include all sorts of things from strange, crispy constructions of tortillas filled with meat, cheese, vegetables, and peppers, to—well, all sorts of things. It seems that no two Mexican restaurants can agree on just what a quesadilla should be, but *usually* you will find that cheese and sour cream are involved.

HUEVOS RANCHEROS:

The all-around best late-night snack and hang-over remedy: fried eggs on a tortilla, sprinkled liberally with salsa (see next item). Because of its medicinal properties and ease of preparation, it is the Mexican food of choice for spring-breakers and the one recipe they attempt back at Midwestern University.

SALSA:

As you may have guessed, this simply means sauce. It is usually made with serrano chili peppers, tomatoes, onions, and cilantro. It may be red or green and it may be served either warm or cold. The best salsa on earth is made with the above ingredients (plus water) ground up in a Mexican mortar (called a *molcajete*). Commercially prepared salsas are also delicious and easy to use.

JALAPENO:

Books have been written about the jalapeño, the National Pepper of Texas. This unassuming little green pepper is often served at fast-food establishments. In fact, it is the acid test to separate the tourists from Texans (other—much hotter—peppers separate the Texans from the Mexicans). First-timers should know several things about jalapeños:

1. They are surprisingly hot.

2. The seeds are even hotter.

3. The oil in the pepper contains the hot material, known as capsicum. Since oil and water don't mix, you should know that drinking water to cool your mouth doesn't help all that much.

4. Stick to the pickled variety; never, ever eat a dry or unpickled jalapeño. At a Mexican restaurant, you may find one on your plate as a garnish. Leave it there—a raw jalapeño has the wallop of a hand grenade.

5. If you *must* eat the jalapeño, do so after you've finished the fajitas.

FRIJOLES AL CHARRO:
One Mexican side dish you should never pass up. In fact, it's probably the first dish you should order. If it's any good, it means that the rest of the food will be, too. Frijoles, of course, are beans, while *charro* in Spanish means "horseman" or "aristocrat." At a good restaurant, frijoles *al charro* is bean soup with all sorts of terrific things thrown in: ham hock, cilantro, garlic, onions, chopped jalapeño (dry, look out!), and maybe even a piece of bacon.

INDEX